50 plus

Unapologetically embracing life
beyond expectation

Dr Rachael Ann Riley

Copyright @2025 by Rachael Ann Riley LLC

All rights reserved. No part of the book may be reproduced or transmitted in any form or by any means without written permission from the author.

ISBN: 979-8-218-64441-3

Table of Contents

Chapter 1: Redefining Yourself on Your Terms. 1

Chapter 2: The Confidence Code Overcoming Self-Doubt 6

Chapter 3: Body, Mind & Soul – Owning Your Power at Any Age .12

Chapter 4: Discovering Your Why – A Purpose-Driven Life 19

Chapter 5: Reinventing Career & Passion Projects. 25

Chapter 6: Legacy & Impact – Leaving Your Mark 32

Chapter 7: The Joy Mindset – Choosing Happiness Every Day 39

Chapter 8: Relationships That Enrich Your Life 45

Chapter 9: Adventure, Travel & Trying New Things. 52

Final Chapter: Your Best Chapter 58

Begins Now 58

Chapter 1

Redefining Yourself on Your Terms

Breaking Free & Embracing Who You Are Meant to Be

Introduction: A New Chapter Begins

Turning 50 and beyond isn't the end of the story—it's the beginning of an entirely new chapter. Yet, many women feel a sense of uncertainty during this phase. Society often sends mixed messages: "Slow down," "You've done enough," or "It's too late to start over." But what if, instead, this was the moment to step fully into who you are meant to be?

Redefining yourself after 50 means rejecting outdated narratives about aging and embracing your own definition of success, fulfillment, and joy. In this chapter, we'll explore how to shed limiting beliefs, step into your power, and craft a life that aligns with your values, desires, and dreams.

The Power of Reinvention: It's Never Too Late

There's a common misconception that personal transformation is reserved for the young. The truth? Some of the world's most inspiring figures found their greatest success later in life:

Vera Wang didn't design her first dress until she was 40.

Colonel Sanders started KFC in his 60s.
Maya Angelou published her first autobiography at 41, launching an iconic literary career.

Julia Child didn't become a famous chef until nearly 50.

If they could redefine their paths, so can you. The key? Shifting your mindset from "I'm too old for this" to "What's next for me?"

Case Study #1

From Homemaker to Bestselling Author

Meet Linda: A Woman Who Refused to Fade Into the Background

Linda, 53, spent decades as a dedicated wife and mother. When her youngest child left for college, she felt lost. For years, her identity had been wrapped up in family obligations. Who was she without them?

Instead of succumbing to the empty nest syndrome, Linda revisited a childhood dream—writing. She joined a local writing group, took online courses, and committed to writing every day. At 55, she self-published her first book. Within a year, she became a bestselling author, proving that it's never too late to follow your passions.

Lesson: Your identity isn't fixed. You can redefine yourself at any time by reconnecting with old passions or discovering new ones.

Shedding Limiting Beliefs & Rewriting Your Narrative

Many women unknowingly carry limiting beliefs that hold them back from stepping into their full potential. Some common ones include:

"I'm too old to start over."

- **Truth:** Experience is an asset, not a limitation. You bring wisdom, skills, and resilience that younger people don't have.

"People will think I'm crazy for changing paths now."

- **Truth:** People will always have opinions, but what matters is how you feel about your own choices.

"I don't know where to start."

- **Truth:** No one has all the answers in the beginning. The key is to take the first step, no matter how small.

Action Step: Write down three beliefs that have been holding you back. Then, challenge each one with a positive truth that empowers you to move forward.

Case Study #2

Career Shift at 58 – From Corporate VP to Wellness Coach
Meet Sandra: Turning Burnout into a New Beginning

At 58, Sandra had spent over 30 years in a demanding corporate role. She was financially secure but emotionally drained. She felt disconnected from her work and yearned for something more fulfilling.

Rather than staying stuck in a job that no longer served her, Sandra leaned into her passion for wellness. She enrolled in a health coaching program, launched an online platform, and began helping midlife women reclaim their vitality. By 60, she had a thriving coaching business, proving that passion and purpose don't have an expiration date.

Lesson: If your career no longer fulfills you, midlife is the perfect time to pivot. With experience, network connections, and a renewed sense of purpose, you can create something new.

Actionable Advice: Steps to Redefine Yourself on Your Terms

Self-Reflection Exercise:

Ask yourself: What do I truly enjoy? What excites me?

Write down three things you've always wanted to do but never pursued. Embrace the Beginner's Mindset:

Give yourself permission to be a beginner. Whether it's starting a blog, learning a language, or launching a business, allow yourself to learn without pressure.

Curate Your Environment for Growth:

Surround yourself with supportive people who encourage change. Join groups, find mentors, or connect with like-minded individuals online.

Create a Personal Manifesto:

Write a declaration of who you are becoming. Example: "I am a woman of purpose, resilience, and courage. I embrace change and step into my future with confidence."

Take Action—One Step at a Time:

Don't wait for the "perfect moment." Start now, whether it's taking a class, applying for a new opportunity, or reaching out to someone in your desired field.

Conclusion: Your Next Chapter Begins Today

Redefining yourself after 50 isn't about chasing youth—it's about embracing your power, wisdom, and dreams on your own terms. Your age isn't a limitation; it's a launching pad for a richer, more fulfilling life.

What's one bold step you can take today to start redefining yourself? Write it down, commit to it, and step forward with confidence. Your best chapter is yet to be written.

Reflection Questions:

What areas of my life do I want to redefine?

What's one belief I need to let go of to step into my new identity?

What's one action I can take this week to move closer to the life I desire?

This is just the beginning of your transformation. The next chapter? Building unstoppable confidence to own your power at every stage of life. Let's dive in!

Chapter 2

The Confidence Code Overcoming Self-Doubt

Breaking Free from Fear & Stepping into Your Power

Introduction: Confidence Is Built, Not Born

Confidence is often mistaken for something you either have or don't. In reality, it's a skill—a muscle that grows stronger with intentional action. For many women over 50, self-doubt can creep in, fueled by societal expectations, past failures, or fear of starting over.

But here's the truth: It's never too late to build unshakable confidence.

In this chapter, we'll uncover the root causes of self-doubt, learn from powerful case studies of women who defied their insecurities, and develop actionable strategies to step into your most confident self.

The Root of Self-Doubt: Why Do We Hold Ourselves Back?

Self-doubt isn't random—it stems from deeply ingrained beliefs and past experiences. Common sources include:

- **Fear of failure** – "What if I try and it doesn't work?"
- **Comparison trap** – "She's so much more successful than me."
- **Perfectionism** – "If I can't do it perfectly, I won't do it at all."

- **Negative past experiences** – "I failed before, so I'll fail again."

The good news? None of these define your future. The first step to overcoming self-doubt is recognizing where it comes from and actively rewriting the narrative.

Case Study #1

From Timid Speaker to Inspirational Leader

Meet Karen: Owning Her Voice at 56

For most of her life, Karen avoided public speaking. She had brilliant ideas but feared judgment. After retiring, she wanted to start a nonprofit for domestic abuse survivors but doubted she could lead.

Instead of giving in to fear, she took action. She joined a local Toastmasters group, practiced speaking in front of small audiences, and sought mentorship.

By 58, Karen confidently led workshops, inspiring hundreds of women. Her organization flourished, proving that confidence is built through action, not just wishful thinking.

Lesson: Confidence isn't about being fearless—it's about acting despite fear.

The Science of Confidence: Rewiring Your Brain

Neuroscience shows that confidence is shaped by repeated behavior. The more you challenge yourself, the more your brain rewires itself to believe in your abilities.

Neuroplasticity means your brain can change at any age.

- **Repetition builds belief** – Every time you act despite self-doubt, you strengthen confidence.

- **Small wins matter** – Even tiny steps create momentum.

Action Step: Instead of waiting to feel confident, take one small bold action today.

Case Study #2

Career Pivot at 60 – From Employee to Entrepreneur

Meet Lisa: From Invisible to Empowered

Lisa spent 30 years in corporate HR. At 60, she wanted to start her own coaching business but felt "too old" and "not expert enough."

Instead of letting doubt win, Lisa:

Started small by offering free coaching to build confidence.

Learned new skills through online courses.

Surrounded herself with supportive mentors.

By 62, she had a thriving coaching business, proving that confidence grows when you take action despite fear.

Lesson: You don't need confidence to start—you build confidence by starting.

Actionable Advice: How to Overcome Self-Doubt & Build Confidence

1. Challenge the Inner Critic

Your inner voice can either build you up or tear you down. When self-doubt creeps in, ask:

Is this fear based on facts or assumptions?

What would I tell a friend in this situation?

What's the worst that can happen—and how would I handle it?

Rewrite negative thoughts:

"I'm not good enough." → "I am learning and growing every day."

2. Take Small, Bold Actions

Confidence comes from doing—not waiting.

Want to start speaking? Volunteer for a small presentation.

Thinking of changing careers? Take one course or talk to someone in your desired field.

Nervous about networking? Reach out to one new person this week.

Every action you take proves to your brain that you are capable.

3. Shift from Perfectionism to Progress

Perfectionism fuels self-doubt because it makes you believe you're never "ready." Instead:

Embrace imperfection – Done is better than perfect.

Set small, achievable goals – One step at a time.

Celebrate progress – Every step forward is a win.

4. Surround Yourself with Confidence Builders

Confidence is contagious. Who you spend time with affects your mindset.

Seek out supportive communities – Join women's groups, masterminds, or mentorship circles.

Limit time with energy-drainers – Avoid those who reinforce self-doubt.
Find expanders – Connect with women who have done what you aspire to do.

5. Create a Confidence Ritual

Develop daily habits that reinforce self-belief:

Morning affirmations – "I am capable. I am enough."

Power poses – Stand tall, shoulders back. Your body influences your brain.

Daily wins journal – Write down one success each day.

Conclusion: Confidence is a Choice—Choose It Daily

Confidence isn't about knowing all the answers—it's about trusting yourself enough to take action. Self-doubt will always whisper in the background, but you don't have to let it control your life.

What bold step will you take today to rewrite your confidence story?

Reflection Questions:

What is one area where self-doubt has been holding you back?

What small step can you take this week to challenge that doubt?

What is one belief about yourself that you need to change to build confidence?

Your transformation starts NOW. In the next chapter, we'll explore how to embrace body, mind, and soul to truly step into your power. Let's go!

Chapter 3

Body, Mind & Soul – Owning Your Power at Any Age

Aligning Your Whole Self for Unshakable Confidence

Introduction: The Power of Wholeness

Confidence isn't just about how you think—it's about how you feel in your body, mind, and soul. When these three elements align, you radiate self-assurance, resilience, and purpose. But too often, women over 50 are told to shrink—to hide wrinkles, to accept slowing down, to fade into the background.

Not anymore.

This chapter is about reclaiming your power in every aspect of your life—physically, mentally, and spiritually. You'll learn how to nurture your body with strength, fuel your mind with positivity, and connect with your soul's deepest purpose.

Section 1

The Body – Strength, Vitality & Self-Love

Redefining Beauty & Strength After 50

Society tells women that youth equals beauty, but true beauty is vitality, confidence, and self-care. Owning your power in your body means:

- Honoring what your body has carried you through.
- Fueling it with the care and respect it deserves.
- Rejecting outdated beauty standards and creating your own.

Case Study

From Unhealthy to Empowered at 57

Meet Maria: A Fitness Journey That Changed More Than Her Body

At 57, Maria had spent years putting everyone else first—her children, her job, her aging parents. One day, after feeling winded from walking up the stairs, she realized she was neglecting herself.

She didn't embark on an extreme fitness journey; instead, she made small, consistent changes:

- Started walking 10 minutes a day.
- Cut back on processed foods and drank more water.
- Began strength training twice a week.

By 58, Maria was stronger, more confident, and more energetic than she had been in years. The best part? It wasn't just about looking good—it was about feeling unstoppable.

Actionable Advice: How to Reclaim Your Body's Power

Move daily – Find a movement you enjoy (walking, yoga, dancing, lifting weights).

Fuel wisely – Eat foods that give you energy and nourishment.

Rest and recover – Sleep is your superpower; aim for 7-9 hours.

Celebrate your body – Stop criticizing it and start appreciating what it does for you.

Affirmation: My body is strong, capable, and worthy of care at every stage of life.

Section 2

The Mind – Rewriting Your Mental Script

The Power of Thought: Your Mind Creates Your Reality

What you tell yourself matters. If you constantly think, I'm too old, I can't do this, I'm not enough, you're reinforcing a cycle of doubt. Instead, retrain your mind to focus on possibilities, strengths, and opportunities.

Case Study

Reinventing Career at 62 with a Growth Mindset

Meet Diane: From Retired Educator to Published Author

Diane retired from teaching at 60 but felt unfulfilled. She had always dreamed of writing a book, but self-doubt whispered, "You're too old to start now." Instead of listening to that voice, she flipped the script:

- "I have wisdom and stories to share."
- "Writing is a skill I can develop."
- "I don't have to be perfect—I just have to start."

She wrote for 30 minutes a day, joined a writing group, and by 62, she published her first book. Now, she's a successful author, proving that your mindset determines your future.

Actionable Advice: How to Strengthen Your Mind's Power

Identify negative thoughts – Write them down, then rewrite them in a positive way.

Surround yourself with positive influences – Books, podcasts, and people who uplift you.

Practice gratitude daily – Focusing on what you have creates abundance thinking.

Learn something new – A new skill or hobby keeps your brain sharp and engaged.

Affirmation: I am capable of growth, change, and endless possibilities.

Section 3

The Soul – Finding Meaning & Inner Peace

Connecting with Your Inner Self

Confidence isn't just external—it's deeply tied to your sense of purpose and fulfillment. When you nurture your soul, you:

- Feel a greater sense of peace and direction.
- Let go of the need for validation from others.
- Step into a life that feels authentic and meaningful.

Case Study

How Susan Found Purpose in Giving Back

Meet Susan: From Emptiness to Fulfillment Through Service

At 54, Susan felt restless. Her children were grown, her career was stable, but something was missing. After reflecting on what brought her joy, she realized she loved mentoring young women.

She started volunteering at a nonprofit, mentoring young professionals, and speaking about confidence and leadership. Suddenly, her life felt rich with purpose again.

Now, at 60, she runs her own mentorship program, proving that serving others can bring the deepest joy.

Actionable Advice: How to Nurture Your Soul's Power

Explore what brings you joy – What makes you lose track of time? Do more of that.

Practice stillness – Whether it's meditation, prayer, or nature walks, give yourself space to listen to your inner voice.

Give back – Helping others connects you to something bigger than yourself. Trust your journey – Life is always evolving. Embrace the unknown with faith.

Affirmation: I am aligned with my purpose, and my soul shines brightly at every stage of life.

Conclusion: The Power of Alignment

When your body, mind, and soul work together, you become unstoppable. Confidence radiates from within—not from external validation but from knowing who you are and what you're capable of.

Reflection Questions:

What is one thing I can do this week to honor my body?

What negative thought do I need to replace with a positive one?

What activity or cause lights up my soul? How can I do more of it?

Next Chapter: Discovering Your Why – A Purpose-Driven Life

Now that you've built the foundation of confidence, it's time to explore your deeper purpose. In the next chapter, we'll dive into discovering your why, uncovering your unique gifts, and aligning your life with what truly matters.

Your journey to owning your power is just beginning—let's keep going!

Chapter 4

Discovering Your Why – A Purpose-Driven Life

Uncovering Your True Calling & Living with Intention

Introduction: The Power of Purpose

What gets you out of bed in the morning? What excites you, fuels you, and gives your life meaning? For many women, especially after 50, there comes a time when they ask: What's next?

Maybe you've raised children, built a career, or checked off societal expectations—but now, it's time for you.

Discovering your why means uncovering the deeper purpose that drives you. It's never too late to realign with your passions, redefine success, and step into your highest calling.

In this chapter, you'll learn how to find your why, see inspiring examples of women who reinvented themselves, and take actionable steps to live a purpose-driven life.

Section 1

Why Purpose Matters – The Science of a Meaningful Life

Studies show that people with a strong sense of purpose:

- Experience greater happiness and fulfillment
- Live longer, healthier lives
- Are more resilient in the face of challenges

Purpose gives your life direction and meaning—it's what makes you feel alive, valuable, and fulfilled.

Case Study #1

From Retirement to Passionate Advocate

Meet Angela: Finding Her Purpose in Community Service

Angela, 60, had just retired from a 35-year teaching career. Instead of feeling relieved, she felt lost. Her job had been her identity for so long—without it, she wasn't sure what her life's purpose was anymore.

One day, she volunteered at a literacy program for underserved women. That single act lit a fire inside her. She started mentoring women, organizing community workshops, and eventually founded a nonprofit to support adult education.

Now, at 65, Angela is more fulfilled than ever, proving that your purpose doesn't retire just because you do.

Lesson: Your why may evolve over time. Stay open to new opportunities that align with your passions.

Section 2

Uncovering Your Why – The 3-Step Process

If you're unsure about your purpose, don't worry—it's already inside you. You just need to uncover it.

Step 1: Reflect on Your Passions & Strengths

Ask yourself:

- What activities make me lose track of time?
- What do people come to me for advice on?
- What problems do I feel passionate about solving?

Actionable Exercise:

Write down 5 things you love doing and 5 skills you're naturally good at. Look for connections.

Step 2: Identify Your Impact

Your purpose is often tied to how you serve others. Think about:

- Who do I feel called to help?
- How can my experiences inspire or support others?

Actionable Exercise:

Write a short statement: "I feel most fulfilled when I _____ because it allows me to _____."

Example: "I feel most fulfilled when I mentor young women because it allows me to give back and share my experiences."

Step 3: Take Small Purpose-Driven Actions

Many women wait for a "grand" purpose to appear. Start small.

Passionate about writing? Start a blog.

Love mentoring? Offer guidance to someone in your community.

Want to help others? Volunteer at a local organization.

Actionable Exercise:

Write down one small step you can take this week toward living your purpose.

Case Study #2

Midlife Reinvention – From Executive to Life Coach

Meet Michelle: Aligning Passion with Purpose

At 55, Michelle had spent decades climbing the corporate ladder. She was financially secure but felt disconnected from her work. She asked herself: If I had no limitations, what would I do?

The answer? Help other women build confidence.

She enrolled in a coaching certification program, started speaking at women's events, and by 57, she was a full-time life coach, transforming lives.

Lesson: Purpose isn't about job titles—it's about doing what lights you up and impacts others.

Section 3: Turning Purpose into a Lifestyle

Once you've identified your why, live it daily.

1. Set Purpose-Driven Goals

Instead of generic goals, ask: Does this align with my deeper purpose?

Instead of: "I want to make more money."
→ Try: "I want to create financial freedom so I can focus on my passion for helping others."

Actionable Exercise: Write one goal that aligns with your why.

2. Surround Yourself with Purpose-Driven People

Seek mentors who inspire you.

Join communities that align with your passions.

Avoid energy-drainers who make you doubt yourself.

Actionable Exercise: Reach out to one person who is living their purpose and learn from them.

3. Embrace Growth & Change

Your purpose will evolve. Stay flexible and open to new paths.

Affirmation: I embrace change and trust that my purpose is unfolding exactly as it should.

Conclusion: Your Purpose-Driven Life Starts Now

Your why is already inside you. It's not about finding something new—it's about uncovering what has always been there.

Reflection Questions:

What makes me feel deeply fulfilled?

How can I use my experiences to help others?

What small step can I take this week to live more purposefully?

Next Chapter: Reinventing Career & Passion Projects

Now that you've discovered your why, let's explore how to turn it into exciting new career opportunities and passion projects. Your purpose doesn't have to stay a dream—it can become your reality.

Your best years are ahead of you—let's make them count!

Chapter 5

Reinventing Career & Passion Projects

Turning Purpose into Opportunity

Introduction: The Power of Midlife Reinvention

Reinvention isn't just possible after 50—it's essential. Gone are the days when turning 50 meant slowing down or settling. Today, women are launching businesses, starting new careers, and exploring passion projects with more confidence, wisdom, and freedom than ever before.

Whether you're looking to switch careers, start a business, or dive into a long-lost passion, this chapter will guide you through how to align your purpose with work that excites you.

You're not too old. You're just getting started.

Section 1

Overcoming Fears About Reinvention

Many women hesitate to reinvent themselves because of limiting beliefs:

"I'm too old to start over."

- **Truth:** Your experience is your greatest asset.

"What if I fail?"
- **Truth:** Every great success story started with uncertainty.

"I don't know where to begin."
- **Truth:** Every new journey starts with a single step.

Case Study

From Lawyer to Holistic Wellness Coach at 58

Meet Janet: A Career Pivot That Changed Lives

At 58, Janet had spent over 30 years as a corporate lawyer. Despite financial success, she felt unfulfilled. She had always been passionate about holistic wellness but never pursued it seriously.

Instead of ignoring her calling, she:

- Took an online certification course in wellness coaching.
- Started coaching friends and colleagues for free.
- Created a website and social media presence.

By 60, Janet had left law behind and built a thriving wellness business. Her passion became her career, proving it's never too late to pivot.

Lesson: You don't have to start over from scratch—you can evolve using your existing skills and passions.

Section 2

Identifying the Right Career or Passion Project for You

Not sure what to pursue? Ask yourself

- What do I enjoy doing so much that I'd do it for free?
- What skills have I mastered that I can share with others?
- How can I turn my expertise into something meaningful?

Actionable Exercise: Write down three potential career paths or projects that excite you.

Turning a Passion into a Career or Side Hustle

If you have a passion, consider these career paths:

1. **Coaching or Consulting** – Use your expertise to guide others (life coaching, career coaching, wellness consulting).

2. **Writing & Publishing** – Share your knowledge through books, blogs, or newsletters.

3. **Public Speaking & Workshops** – Teach, inspire, and lead events.

4. **E-Commerce & Product Creation** – Sell handmade goods, courses, or digital products.

5. **Nonprofit & Philanthropy** – Create impact through community work.

Actionable Exercise: Pick one idea and brainstorm 3 steps to get started.

Section 3

Building Confidence to Take the Leap

Case Study

From Teacher to Online Course Creator at 55

Meet Lisa: Turning Decades of Experience into an Online Business

Lisa had been a schoolteacher for 30 years. When she retired, she wanted to continue impacting lives but in a new way. She realized she could:

- Package her knowledge into an online course for educators.
- Teach workshops and webinars from home.
- Earn passive income while making a difference.

Within a year, Lisa's online courses were bringing in steady income. She turned her expertise into a thriving business.

Lesson: You don't have to start from scratch—you can monetize what you already know.

Actionable Exercise: Write down one skill you have that others would pay to learn.

Section 4

Practical Steps to Reinvent Your Career or Passion Project

1. Invest in Learning & Growth

Take an online course or certification.

Read books or listen to podcasts on your industry.

Connect with mentors who've already done what you want to do.

Actionable Exercise: Find one learning resource and commit to studying it this month.

2. Build Your Brand & Visibility

Update your LinkedIn profile and resume.

Create a personal website or portfolio.

Use social media to share your expertise.

Actionable Exercise: Start one online platform (LinkedIn, a blog, or an Instagram page).

3. Start Small & Gain Experience

Offer your services for free or at a discount to build credibility.

Volunteer or intern in your new field.

Start a side hustle before fully transitioning.

Actionable Exercise: Find one way to gain hands-on experience in your new field.

4. Network & Find Support

Join industry groups, masterminds, or networking events.

Connect with people doing what you aspire to do.

Seek out mentors and accountability partners.

Actionable Exercise: Reach out to one new person in your desired field this week.

Conclusion: Your Reinvention Starts Today

Reinvention isn't about changing who you are—it's about becoming more of who you're meant to be.

Reflection Questions:

What career or passion project excites me the most?

What's one small step I can take this week to move toward reinvention?

What limiting belief do I need to let go of to move forward?

Next Chapter: Legacy & Impact – Leaving Your Mark

Now that you're reinventing your career and passions, it's time to think bigger. How do you want to be remembered? In the next chapter, we'll explore how to build a lasting impact through mentorship, philanthropy, and legacy-building.

Your best years are ahead—let's make them extraordinary.

Chapter 6

Legacy & Impact – Leaving Your Mark

Creating a Life That Inspires and Endures

Introduction: What Will You Be Remembered For?

At this stage in life, many women begin thinking beyond personal success. They ask deeper questions:

What kind of impact am I making?

How will I be remembered?

How can I leave a lasting legacy?

Legacy isn't just about wealth or accomplishments—it's about the lives you touch, the wisdom you share, and the impact you create. In this chapter, we'll explore how to build a legacy of purpose, whether through mentorship, philanthropy, storytelling, or community service.

Your best years aren't just about living for yourself—they're about leaving a mark that lasts.

Section 1

Defining Your Legacy

Legacy isn't just something you leave behind when you pass away—it's the way you live right now.

- It's the values you instill in your children and community.
- It's the wisdom and experience you share.
- It's the kindness, love, and leadership you embody.

Case Study

The Woman Who Built a Generational Legacy

Meet Eleanor: Teaching Financial Freedom to Future Generations

Eleanor, 61, was raised in a family that struggled financially. She made it her mission to break the cycle for her grandchildren.

Instead of just leaving money behind, she taught her family how to build wealth:

- She started a financial literacy program for young women.
- She mentored her grandchildren on saving, investing, and entrepreneurship.
- She created a foundation to support single mothers in financial hardship.

Now, Eleanor's impact will outlive her, not just through her family, but through every life she's helped transform.

Lesson: Legacy is about more than material wealth—it's about teaching, inspiring, and empowering others.

Actionable Exercise: Write down three values or lessons you want to pass on to future generations.

Section 2

Mentorship – Guiding the Next Generation

One of the most powerful ways to leave a legacy is through mentorship. You have a lifetime of wisdom, experience, and lessons learned—now is the time to share them.

- **Become a mentor** – Guide young professionals or entrepreneurs.
- **Support women in transition** – Help those going through career changes, divorce, or personal struggles.
- **Teach what you know** – Offer workshops, coaching, or write about your experiences.

Case Study

From Corporate CEO to Leadership Mentor

Meet Sandra: Leading the Next Generation of Women Entrepreneurs

After retiring at 55, Sandra felt restless. She didn't want to start another business, but she wasn't ready to stop making a difference.

She began mentoring young women in leadership and helping them launch their own businesses.

Within three years, Sandra had:

- Helped 15 women start their own successful companies.
- Developed an online course for female entrepreneurs.
- Hosted leadership retreats for women over 40.

Lesson: Legacy isn't just about what you build—it's about who you lift up along the way.
Actionable Exercise: Identify one person you can mentor or support in their journey.

Section 3

Giving Back Through Philanthropy & Service

Philanthropy doesn't mean donating millions—it means using what you have to serve others.

Ways to give back:

- **Volunteer** – Serve at nonprofits, schools, or community projects.
- **Create a foundation** – Support a cause you believe in.
- **Start a social initiative** – Lead a movement for change.
- **Offer pro bono work** – Share your skills for free to those in need.

Case Study

A Businesswoman's Legacy of Giving

Meet Ruth: Turning Business Success Into a Mission

At 62, Ruth had a thriving fashion brand. But instead of just growing profits, she wanted to use her business for good.

She created a program to train and employ women from underserved communities in fashion design. Today, her brand isn't just successful—it's changing lives.

Lesson: Legacy isn't just about success—it's about using success to create real change.

Actionable Exercise: Choose one cause you care about and find a way to contribute.

Section 4

Storytelling – Preserving Your Wisdom & Experiences

Your story is part of your legacy. Whether through writing, speaking, or sharing experiences, your words have the power to inspire future generations.

Ways to share your story:

- **Write a memoir or blog** – Document your experiences and lessons.
- **Record video messages** – Share life advice with your family and community.
- **Speak publicly** – Inspire others through storytelling.

Case Study

The Woman Who Shared Her Story & Changed Lives

Meet Deborah: From Pain to Purpose

Deborah, 58, had survived domestic abuse and spent years healing. She knew her story could help others, so she:

- Wrote a book about her journey.
- Started speaking at women's empowerment events.
- Created a nonprofit for survivors.

Her words gave hope to thousands, proving that your story—no matter how painful—can be part of someone else's healing and transformation.

Lesson: Never underestimate the power of your voice and experiences.

Actionable Exercise: Write down one life lesson you want to share with others.

Conclusion: Your Legacy Begins Today

Legacy isn't something you leave behind when you're gone—it's something you create every day through your actions, words, and impact.

Reflection Questions:

What do I want to be remembered for?

How can I start making a difference today?

What story, wisdom, or experience can I share with others?

Next Chapter: The Joy Mindset – Choosing Happiness Every Day

Now that you've aligned with purpose, let's explore how to cultivate daily joy and fulfillment. Confidence, purpose, and legacy mean nothing if you're not truly enjoying the journey.

Your best years aren't behind you—they're waiting to be fully lived. Let's embrace joy, gratitude, and happiness in the next chapter.

Chapter 7

The Joy Mindset – Choosing Happiness Every Day

Cultivating Daily Joy, Gratitude, and Fulfillment

Introduction: Joy is a Choice, Not Just a Feeling

Happiness isn't something that happens to you—it's something you cultivate. Joy is a mindset, a decision, and a practice.

After 50, many women experience shifts—children leave home, careers change, relationships evolve. These transitions can feel unsettling, but they also present an opportunity: the chance to redefine happiness on your terms.

This chapter will explore how to create a joy-filled life every day, no matter your circumstances. You'll learn how to cultivate gratitude, let go of negativity, and find deep fulfillment in life's simple moments.

Section 1

Understanding the Science of Happiness

Research shows that happiness isn't about wealth, youth, or external achievements—it's about how you think and live.

- Gratitude rewires your brain for positivity.
- Acts of kindness boost serotonin and create fulfillment.
- Mindfulness and presence reduce stress and increase joy.

Case Study

The Woman Who Chose Joy Over Circumstances

Meet Linda: Finding Happiness After Loss

At 55, Linda lost her husband unexpectedly. Grief consumed her, and for months, she struggled to see any light. But one day, she made a decision:

- Every morning, she wrote one thing she was grateful for.
- She started volunteering at a local children's shelter.
- She took a solo trip to Italy, something she had always dreamed of doing.

By 58, Linda found herself smiling more, laughing often, and embracing life again. She realized that happiness wasn't about avoiding pain—it was about choosing joy despite it.

Lesson: Life is unpredictable, but joy is always a choice.

Actionable Exercise: Write down three things you're grateful for every morning for the next week.

Section 2

Letting Go of Negativity & Stress

To make space for joy, you must release what drains your energy:

- **Comparison** – Stop measuring your life against others.
- **Regret** – Let go of "should haves" and embrace the present.
- **Toxic relationships** – Surround yourself with people who lift you up.

Case Study

A Woman Who Walked Away from Stress

Meet Deborah: From Stressful Career to Peaceful Living

At 57, Deborah was exhausted from decades of a high-pressure career. She had money, but no time for joy.

Instead of waiting for "someday," she made a bold move:

- She downsized her lifestyle to reduce financial pressure.
- She moved to a beach town and started a small, fulfilling business.
- She prioritized slow mornings, nature walks, and time with loved ones.

Now, at 60, Deborah says she's never been happier—not because she works less, but because she prioritizes joy.

Lesson: Less stress = more room for happiness.

Actionable Exercise: Identify one stressful thing you can remove from your life this week.

Section 3

Finding Joy in the Simple Things

Happiness isn't about big achievements—it's in the small, everyday moments:

- A cup of coffee in the morning.
- A walk in the sunshine.
- A deep conversation with a friend.

Case Study

A 63-Year-Old Who Redefined Happiness

Meet Carol: Discovering Joy in Simplicity

Carol spent years chasing career milestones, thinking each achievement would make her happier. But at 63, she realized:

- Joy wasn't in external success—it was in the present moment.
- She started gardening, painting, and spending time with her grandkids.
- She slowed down and began truly enjoying life.

Now, Carol says she's more fulfilled than she ever was during her high-powered career.

Lesson: Joy isn't in the extraordinary—it's in the ordinary moments we embrace.

Actionable Exercise: Pause right now and write down three simple things that bring you joy.

Section 4

Cultivating a Daily Joy Practice

1. Practice Daily Gratitude

Science-backed happiness booster – Start your day with three things you're grateful for.

Exercise: Keep a gratitude journal and write in it for one minute every morning.

2. Move Your Body with Love

Exercise isn't just for fitness—it boosts endorphins and joy.

Exercise: Find one joyful movement (dancing, yoga, walking) and do it daily.

3. Surround Yourself with Joyful People

Energy is contagious—be around people who inspire and uplift you.

Exercise: Call or meet one person this week who brings you joy.

4. Do More of What Makes You Feel Alive

Identify the activities that energize you and do them more often.

Exercise: Pick one passion to spend time on this week.

Conclusion: Joy is Your Birthright

Happiness isn't about waiting for the perfect moment—it's about choosing joy daily, despite imperfections.

Reflection Questions:

What is one small habit I can adopt to create more joy?

What stress or negativity do I need to let go of?

What simple pleasure do I need to slow down and enjoy more?

Next Chapter: Relationships That Enrich Your Life

Now that you've learned to cultivate joy, let's explore how to build meaningful, fulfilling relationships. Because happiness is even greater when shared.

Your happiest years are still ahead—let's embrace them fully.

Chapter 8

Relationships That Enrich Your Life

Nurturing Meaningful Connections & Letting Go of Toxic Ties

Introduction: The Power of Connection

At every stage of life, relationships shape our experiences. The quality of our friendships, romantic partnerships, and social circles has a direct impact on our happiness and well-being.

After 50, many women go through major relationship shifts—children move out, friendships evolve, marriages change, or new connections form. This chapter is about intentionally cultivating relationships that bring joy, support, and deep connection while letting go of those that drain or no longer serve you.

You deserve relationships that make you feel seen, valued, and uplifted.

Section 1

Evaluating Your Relationships – Who Adds & Who Drains?

Not all relationships are meant to last forever. As you evolve, so should the people around you.

Signs of Healthy, Life-Enriching Relationships

- Mutual respect and support
- Shared joy and laughter
- Honest communication
- Feeling energized after interactions

Signs of Toxic or Draining Relationships

- Constant negativity or drama
- Feeling unappreciated or unheard
- Being used for emotional or financial support
- Fear of speaking your truth

Case Study

How Lisa Let Go of Toxic Friendships & Found Her Tribe

At 54, Lisa realized that many of her long-time friendships were one-sided and emotionally exhausting.

- She stopped overcommitting to people who never reciprocated.
- She set boundaries with energy-draining friends.
- She joined a local women's empowerment group and found uplifting, like-minded women.

Now, at 57, Lisa says she's surrounded by people who genuinely support and inspire her.

Lesson: Not everyone is meant to stay in your life forever—and that's okay.

Actionable Exercise: Write down three people in your life who uplift you and three who drain you. Reflect on how to invest more in the positive ones.

Section 2

Strengthening Friendships That Matter

Friendships in midlife can be some of the deepest and most rewarding because they're built on shared experiences, mutual respect, and genuine connection.

Ways to Strengthen Friendships:

- **Make time for connection** – Schedule regular meetups or calls.
- **Be intentional about communication** – Express appreciation and check in.
- **Support each other's dreams** – Celebrate wins and be there in tough times.

Case Study

How Two Women Built a Lifelong Sisterhood

At 60, Janet and Maria met at a yoga class. What started as small talk turned into a deep sisterhood of support.

- They travel together once a year.
- They set monthly "check-in" coffee dates.
- They encourage each other to pursue passions and goals.

Today, at 65, they say their friendship is stronger than ever—proof that it's never too late to find your people.

Lesson: Invest in the friendships that make you feel seen and valued.

Actionable Exercise: Reach out to one friend today and schedule time to connect.

Section 3

Cultivating Romantic Relationships – Whether New or Renewed

For Those in Relationships: Keeping Love Alive After 50

Long-term relationships evolve. The key to keeping them fulfilling is intention and effort.

Ways to Rekindle Connection:

- **Prioritize quality time** – Date nights, travel, or shared hobbies.
- **Communicate openly** – Express needs, desires, and appreciation.
- **Try new experiences together** – Keep excitement alive with adventures.

Case Study

How Sarah & John Reignited Their Marriage After 30 Years

At 58, Sarah and John realized they had fallen into routine—they were more roommates than partners.

- They started a weekly "no phone" dinner tradition.
- They took a dance class together.
- They planned a bucket-list vacation.

By 60, their relationship felt fresh and exciting again.

Lesson: Love thrives when nurtured with intention.

Actionable Exercise: Plan one new experience with your partner this month.

For Those Seeking New Love: It's Never Too Late

Many women over 50 wonder: Can I still find love? Absolutely.

Keys to Finding Meaningful Love in Midlife:

- **Be open** – Love can come from unexpected places.
- **Know your worth** – Don't settle for less than you deserve.
- **Put yourself out there** – Join groups, events, or try dating apps designed for mature singles.

Case Study

Finding Love at 62 – Janet's Story

Janet, widowed at 58, didn't expect to date again. But at 62, she met someone at a book club. Their shared love of literature turned into a deep romance, proving that love has no expiration date.

Lesson: Love is possible at any age—if you're open to it.

Actionable Exercise: Say yes to one social opportunity this month that could lead to new connections.

Section 4

Building a Community of Support & Sisterhood

How to Expand Your Social Circle & Meet Like-Minded People

- **Join a women's group** – Find local or online communities.
- **Attend social events** – Workshops, retreats, or networking events.
- **Be proactive** – Reach out, invite, and build connections.

Case Study

How Michelle Built a Supportive Community

At 56, Michelle moved to a new city and felt lonely. Instead of waiting for friendships to happen, she:

- Started a monthly book club.
- Attended women's leadership events.
- Hosted small dinner gatherings.

Within a year, she had built a close-knit community that felt like family.

Lesson: If you want connection, take the first step.

Actionable Exercise: Join one new group or event this month to expand your circle.

Conclusion: Relationships Are the Heart of a Joyful Life

The people you surround yourself with shape your happiness. Be intentional about nurturing the relationships that matter and letting go of those that don't.

Reflection Questions:

Who in my life brings me the most joy?

What relationships do I need to invest more in?

What's one step I can take to create more meaningful connections?

Next Chapter: Adventure, Travel & Trying New Things

Now that you've cultivated fulfilling relationships, it's time to embrace new experiences and adventures. The next chapter will explore how to step outside your comfort zone and live boldly.

Your best years are waiting—let's make them unforgettable!

Chapter 9

Adventure, Travel & Trying New Things

Stepping Outside Your Comfort Zone & Embracing New Experiences

Introduction: It's Never Too Late to Explore Life

Many women over 50 feel like their adventurous years are behind them—but the truth is, they're just beginning.

Adventure isn't just about traveling the world (though that's amazing, too). It's about saying yes to new experiences, challenging yourself, and living fully.

In this chapter, we'll explore:

- How to cultivate an adventurous mindset
- Inspiring stories of women who embraced new experiences
- Practical ways to infuse excitement into your life

Your comfort zone is a beautiful place, but nothing ever grows there. It's time to step out and embrace life boldly.

Section 1

The Adventure Mindset – Redefining What's Possible

Adventure is more than just physical experiences—it's a mindset:

- **Curiosity** – Asking, What else is out there for me?
- **Openness** – Saying yes more often.
- **Courage** – Embracing discomfort and uncertainty.

Case Study

How Carol Transformed Her Life at 58

At 58, Carol had never traveled alone. She always waited for the "right time" or the "right companion."

One day, she decided: No more waiting.

- She booked a solo trip to Spain.
- She met incredible people, learned a new language, and fell in love with solo travel.
- By 60, she had visited 10 countries—proving that life doesn't end at 50—it expands.

Lesson: Fear fades when you take action. The first step is always the hardest—after that, it's exhilarating.

Actionable Exercise: Write down one experience you've always wanted to try but haven't yet.

Section 2

Traveling Boldly – Whether Near or Far

1. Traveling Solo – The Ultimate Confidence Booster

Solo travel can be empowering, exciting, and deeply fulfilling.

- You make your own schedule.
- You meet new people.
- You gain independence and confidence.

Tips for Safe & Enjoyable Solo Travel:

- Start with a short trip to build confidence.
- Stay in women-friendly accommodations (Airbnbs, hostels, boutique hotels).
- Join local tours or group activities to meet people.

2. Group Travel – Finding Your Travel Tribe

If solo travel isn't for you, group travel is an amazing alternative.

- Join women's travel groups or retreats.
- Travel with friends or family for bonding experiences.
- Explore volunteer travel opportunities.

Case Study

Janet's First Girls' Trip at 62

At 62, Janet had never traveled with friends. She decided to join a women's travel group to Greece.

- She made lifelong friends.
- She conquered her fear of trying new foods and experiences.
- She realized travel wasn't just about the destination—it was about connection and growth.

Lesson: Adventure is even better when shared. Find your travel tribe!

Actionable Exercise: Research one destination and plan a future trip—solo or with friends.

Section 3

Trying New Things – Breaking Routine & Finding Joy

Adventure isn't just about travel—it's about trying new things in everyday life.

- **Take a class** – Dance, art, cooking, photography.
- **Learn a new skill** – A language, instrument, or craft.
- **Say yes to social invitations** – Meet new people and explore new places.

Case Study

How Sandra Reinvented Herself at 55

Sandra, 55, had never painted before, but she always admired artists.

- She signed up for a beginner's painting class.
- She found it therapeutic and fun.
- By 57, she was selling her artwork and hosting community art nights.

Lesson: New experiences awaken hidden talents and passions.

Actionable Exercise: Choose one new thing to try this month and commit to it.

Section 4

Overcoming Fear & Embracing Uncertainty

Many women hesitate to try new things because of fear:

- What if I fail?
- What if I thrive?
- What if people judge me?
- What if I inspire someone?

How to Overcome Fear & Take the Leap

- **Start small** – Take one step at a time.
- **Embrace discomfort** – Growth happens outside your comfort zone.
- **Celebrate progress** – Every new experience builds confidence.

Case Study: Lisa's First Public Speaking Gig at 59

Lisa, 59, always feared public speaking. But when asked to share her story at a conference, she said yes.

- She practiced with a mentor.
- She focused on impact, not perfection.
- After her first talk, she felt empowered—now she speaks regularly.

Lesson: Fear loses its power when you face it head-on.

Actionable Exercise: Identify one fear that's holding you back. Take a small step toward overcoming it.

Conclusion: Your Best Adventures Are Ahead

Adventure isn't about being reckless—it's about being bold, curious, and open to what life has to offer.

Reflection Questions:

What's one adventure (big or small I want to experience?

How can I add more spontaneity and excitement to my life?
What fear is keeping me from fully living?

Final Chapter: Your Best Chapter Begins Now

This book was never just about confidence—it was about embracing life with purpose, joy, and excitement.

In the final chapter, we'll bring everything together and create an action plan for living wholeheartedly. Because your best years aren't behind you—they're ahead.

Let's step boldly into the future.

Final Chapter

Your Best Chapter Begins Now

Living Wholeheartedly, Fearlessly, and Unapologetically

Introduction: A New Beginning, Not an Ending

You've reached the end of this book—but this is just the beginning of your next chapter.

Throughout these pages, you've explored:

- Redefining yourself on your terms (Chapter 1)
- Building unshakable confidence (Chapter 2)
- Owning your power—body, mind, and soul (Chapter 3)
- Finding purpose and living with meaning (Chapter 4)
- Reinventing your career and passions (Chapter 5)
- Creating a lasting impact and legacy (Chapter 6)
- Choosing joy every single day (Chapter 7)
- Cultivating deep, fulfilling relationships (Chapter 8)
- Embracing adventure and new experiences (Chapter 9)

Now, it's time to take everything you've learned and step into your power.

The question isn't what comes next—the question is:

What will you do with this new, limitless version of yourself?

Section 1

The Wholehearted Living Action Plan

You don't need a grand plan or drastic change to live more fully. Small, intentional steps lead to big transformations.

Step 1: Define Your Wholehearted Living Vision

Ask yourself:

- What does my most fulfilled life look like?
- How do I want to feel every day?
- What is one thing I can do to step closer to that vision?

Actionable Exercise: Write a short vision statement about the life you want to live. Example:

"I am a confident, joyful woman who embraces new experiences, builds meaningful relationships, and shares my wisdom to uplift others. I live with purpose, adventure, and gratitude every day."

Step 2: Set Your Bold, Fearless Goals

Dream big, then take small steps.

- **Personal Growth Goal** – (e.g., Start a new hobby, prioritize self-care, face a fear)
- **Relationship Goal** – (e.g., Strengthen a friendship, set boundaries, meet new people)
- **Purpose Goal** – (e.g., Start a business, write a book, mentor others)
- **Adventure Goal** – (e.g., Travel somewhere new, take a risk, say yes to an opportunity)

Actionable Exercise: Write down one goal in each category.

Step 3: Take Immediate, Inspired Action

The time to act is NOW. No waiting for "someday" or the "perfect time."

- What is one thing you can do today to start living more wholeheartedly?
- Who is one person you can reach out to for encouragement or support?
- What one commitment can you make to yourself?

Actionable Exercise: Write down ONE action you will take this week.

Section 2

Embracing the Unpredictability of Life

Wholehearted living isn't about perfection—it's about being fully present in the highs and lows.

- **You will have setbacks**—but they won't define you.
- **You will experience fear**—but you won't let it stop you.
- **You will evolve**—and that's a beautiful thing.

The goal isn't to have all the answers—it's to keep showing up for yourself.

Section 3

Your Final Call to Action

Case Study

How Lorraine Created Her Best Chapter at 65

Lorraine, 65, spent years thinking it was "too late" to chase her dreams. But when she turned 60, she made a decision:

- She wrote her first book.
- She started traveling solo.
- She built a community of like-minded women.

At 65, she said:

"I used to think my best years were behind me. Now, I realize they were just beginning."

Lesson: The moment you decide to own your power, your whole life changes.
Conclusion: Your Future is Limitless

This isn't just a book—it's a call to action.

You have the power to:

- Live boldly
- Love deeply
- Take risks
- Say YES to new opportunities
- Step into your purpose

Your next chapter isn't written yet—you get to create it.

Reflection Questions:

What will I do differently after reading this book?

What fear am I ready to let go of?

What is the first step I will take to start living wholeheartedly?

Final Words: You Are Enough. You Are Powerful. This is Your Time.

No more waiting. No more doubts. No more settling.

Your best years are happening NOW.

Go live them fully, unapologetically, and wholeheartedly.

Thank you for taking this journey. Now go create the life you were meant to live.

Acknowledgments & Next Steps

If you loved this book, let's stay connected:

- Follow my work for more inspiration
- Join my community for support and sisterhood
- Share your story—I'd love to hear how you're embracing your next chapter!

Keep in touch!

FB Page: Resilience Mastery

IG: @iamrachaelariley.lifecoach
IG: @i_am_enough_my_journey

Website: https://iamenoughmyjourney.com/

Send email to: rae@iamenoughmyjourney.com

Made in the USA
Monee, IL
01 May 2025